Elizabeth's Poetry of Hope

Foreword by

Lord Hague of Richmond

1 3 5 7 9 10 8 6 4 2

First published in 2021 by Elizabeth's Legacy of Hope

Front cover illustration by Kerry Timewell
Typeset by RefineCatch Limited, www.refinecatch.com
Printed and bound in Great Britain by Clays Ltd, Elcograf S.p.A.

ISBN 978-1-3999-1068-2

Elizabeth's Legacy of Hope
Registered Charity Number 1141287
www.elizabethslegacyofhope.org

Contents

Foreword 5

Introduction 7

PART ONE: Poems of Joy 10

PART TWO: Love from Liberia and Sierra Leone, Poetry and Letters 15

PART THREE: Poems of Courage 27

PART FOUR: Inspired by India 37

PART FIVE: Poems to Lighten Darkness 42

PART SIX: Just Wrong 48

PART SEVEN: Poetry by Children, for Children, for whom we all are 49

PART EIGHT: Special Collection – Poetry with Legs, by Patron Ian Whybrow 59

Epilogue 72

Acknowledgements 76

ELIZABETH'S POETRY OF HOPE

Poetry is what in a poem makes you laugh, cry, prickle, be silent, makes your toenails twinkle, makes you want to do this or that or nothing, makes you know that you are alone in the unknown world, that your bliss and suffering is forever shared and forever all your own
– *Dylan Thomas*

Poetry is the rhythmical creation of beauty in words
– *Edgar Allan Poe*

Poetry is the spontaneous overflow of powerful feelings: it takes its origin from emotion recollected in tranquillity – *William Wordsworth*

Poetry is when an emotion has found its thought and the thought has found words – *Robert Frost*

Poetry has been to me its own exceeding great reward; it has given me the habit of wishing to discover the good and beautiful in all that meets and surrounds me
– *Samuel Taylor Coleridge*

Poets are the sense, philosophers the intelligence of humanity – *Samuel Beckett*

Poetry is nearer to vital truth than history – *Plato*

Foreword

by Lord Hague of Richmond

Poetry has a profound power to shed light on some of the darkest aspects of the human condition, not least the devastating impact of war and disease. In my youth, I recall being awed by the emotional impact of Wilfred Owen's "Disabled", a harrowing poem which expresses the pain of a young soldier who lost his limbs in the First World War.

It is a poem that continued to inspire me during my work in Government to support disabled people, first here at home as Social Security Minister and later internationally as Foreign Secretary. As a result of my time in these two roles, I understand the life-changing impact of amputations and the need for greater support to help those adjusting to the loss of limbs.

The World Health Organisation estimates that there are 40 million amputees living in developing countries, with only 5% of them having access to any form of prosthetic care. This failure to support amputees is largely a result of a lack of availability of prosthetics, the cost of such prosthetics, poor awareness, and limited levels of trained personnel.

This lack of health care support is complemented by a lack of social support, with amputees all too often subjected to stigma in their communities. Such stigma is particularly damaging for amputee children, many of whom already suffer from low self-confidence as a result of their injuries. This has a direct impact on their education, with the vast majority of child amputees in the developing world not going to school.

These twin challenges of health care provision and social stigma are why the work of charities such as Elizabeth's Legacy of Hope is so important. Since their launch in 2011, the charity has changed the lives of over 250 vulnerable child amputees, providing them with the mobility and education they need to fulfil their potential. Indeed, they are the only charity working specifically to support child amputees in Sierra Leone and Liberia, making their activities all the more important.

Given the vital work of Elizabeth's Legacy of Hope, and the power of poetry, I am delighted to support this collection of poems, featuring works especially authored by poets and child amputees in developing countries. I hope you will find their words as profoundly moving as I have.

Lord Hague of Richmond

Introduction

by Victoria Panton Bacon, Co-Founder of Elizabeth's Legacy of Hope, with Sarah Hope

"While my joy was being washed away, Elizabeth's Legacy of Hope came knocking. With fresh and new hope to hold unto that I may walk again they built me a prosthesis, and with education they enlighten my hope.

I may not be able to pay back, but the smile on my face shows how grateful I am."

These words are written by seventeen-year-old Ezekiel, from Liberia. When Ezekiel was little more than six, he fell whilst playing on metal bars in his garden that his mother used to dry clothes. The fall was devastating; his left leg broke in four places and within a short time infection set in, and amputation at the hip had to be undertaken to save his young life.

Ezekiel grew up with only his right leg, using crutches so he could at least move around a little bit. There is government provision in countries like Liberia for some child amputees to receive prosthetic support but it has to be paid for and for most families – Ezekiel's included – that makes this vital support impossible to reach.

Ezekiel did learn, as a young child, to use his crutches and he was able – most days – to go to school. However, his childhood was exhausting, physically of course, but also mentally. Before his accident he was a bright, cheerful boy who loved to play with his friends. But after becoming an amputee Ezekiel was shunned and left alone, as was his mother. Their 'society' pointed a cruel finger of blame at both of them, the 'reason' for the accident being they must have done something dreadful during a previous life.

This is wrong, of course. Everything about a child with a disability being mocked for being different is wrong, as it is wrong for that child not to receive the support they need. But this is the cruel reality of life for thousands of amputees in poor, developing and war-torn countries.

Millions of children across the world need extra help to give them the opportunities they deserve, for thousands of different reasons. We can't all help them all, of course, but if the millions of us who can help, do help in a concentrated, well-organised way I do believe that many disadvantaged children, for whom doors are closed through no fault of their own, will find the key they need to open those doors.

This is the hope that Elizabeth's Legacy of Hope seeks to provide; as this book is compiled, we are helping children in Liberia and Sierra Leone in West Africa, and India. In May 2021 we passed our tenth anniversary – over the decade we have helped child amputees in these countries, and in Tanzania too – we are proud of the vital care we have given them and long to help many more. We could not do this without the support of all our donors and supporters, and the caregivers in each of our chosen countries. Thank you to you all.

This poetry book contains poems, and prose, written to tell the story of Elizabeth's Legacy of Hope; words crafted by many published, and some unpublished poets, from around the country. Thank you to all those who have contributed. There are also incredibly special thoughts from the children we help; the poignancy of their words speaks for itself. I hope very much you will enjoy these poems and will find the words uplifting, as they are intended to be.

Elizabeth's Legacy of Hope is a charity born out of a tragedy – the seed of 'hope' for the children we care for was sown on a sunny April morning in London in 2007 when my mother, Elizabeth, was struck by a London bus that killed her. She was with her granddaughter, my niece, Pollyanna Hope, who was then learning to walk, but left an amputee. My twin sister Sarah was with them too, she suffered life-changing injuries. I was in hospital with a two-day old baby. I don't want or need to say anything more about that day, the horror needs not be described but the explanation for how Elizabeth's Legacy of Hope came to be needs to be written. Pollyanna, now a beautiful sixteen-year-old, who has learnt to dance, is our inspiration and every child we help is cared for in Elizabeth's memory.

Quite simply, it was obvious to us, as a family as the days and weeks unfolded after Elizabeth died, that Pollyanna was going to lead a normal and fulfilling life, albeit with extra challenges, because she lives in a developed country and receives the care and prosthetic support she needs.

We believe all child amputees deserve this help. Thank you for supporting us by buying this book, thank you for being part of our journey.

Victoria

PART ONE: Poems of Joy

Sarah, Pollyanna and Victoria

Elizabeth

Hope is a Blanket – by Pollyanna Hope

Hope is blanket that rests on you
Hope is a person who guides you on your way
Hope is a world where people are smiling, there is not a frown to be seen

Courage is a gift that pushes you
To climb to the top of Mount Everest
Courage is the bird that perches on your shoulder when you run into battle
Courage is a lion that follows a yellow brick road
To find his courage

Hope is a flower that blooms into life
Courage is a chick that hatches out of his shell

Where Dreams Begin – by Brian Moses

Everybody's always looking for
that place where dreams end,
but I'm looking out for the place
where dreams begin.

I'm looking for that starting point
where the excitement unravels,
the point where ideas interlink
and travel, tumbling down
from the brain in a waterfall
of possibilities.

That's the place where I like to be
the place where nothing
has yet been attempted
and it's a long way to go
before anything goes wrong.

It's that place where I'm not tied
to earth anymore,
I can let my dreams rise.
Let them soar like a kite
that easily takes flight

And there's nothing to weigh
me down, no warning sound
to hold me back. It's a blank canvas
to which I can pin anything.

Yes, I'm looking for that place
where dreams begin,
I'm looking for my path to the sky

Love's Sacrifice – by Donald Sutthery (late)

Sweet as the moon's tear on the budding rose,
Dear as the kiss I wished, nor thought to gain'
Welcome as heat amid the Arctic snows,
Or as the north wind on the Libyan Plain,
So dear, so sweet, the love I have for thee!

Dearest of all the love that loves for nought!
Sweetest of all the love with nought to gain;
Whole worlds may win the joys by passion taught;
For me and thee, dear heart, the crown of pain!

Proudest of all crowns is my love for thee.

A Magical Dream – Rollo Bacon

Once in the wood of a magical dream I stood
Alone in the dark of the quiet wood
All there was to hear was an owl make a call
And spirits of Endurance were trees that towered high
And spirits of Fellowship were streams that connected
And spirits of Trust were the leaves that grew
And spirits of Love were the stars that shone
And sprits of Peace were the animals that slept
And spirits of Service were the birds that fed chicks
In that magical wood in the land of sleep.

Drop in the Ocean – by Jane Clarke

Sploshing around
in life's restless sea,
there's a drop in the ocean –
and that drop is me.

Surfing the waves,
or washed up on the shore,
I'm a minuscule drop
among zillions more.

I'm a drop in the ocean
of life's restless sea.
But there'd be no ocean
without drops like me!

Sunrise – Debra Bertulis

Look!
Just over the hill
The sky!
The sun is chasing away the grey
I told you it would come

Can you see?
See how it turns
From orange to red to gold
I can see you are weary
Don't close your eyes
Not for a minute
Not for a second, please
Or you will miss this

I told you it would find us
That it was just over the hill
And look!
Here it is
For us
Beautiful, beautiful, beautiful
Hope

A smile after tears – by Jane Clarke

A smile after tears
like sun shining through showers
makes life a rainbow

A Word of Advice, Sunshine – Shauna Darling Robertson

Keep the sun in your pocket
for grey winter days.

If a door slams, don't knock it –
put the sun in your pocket
and be on your way.

Cut the heart loose, don't lock it
but keep the sun in your pocket.

There'll be grey winter days

PART TWO: Love from Liberia and Sierra Leone, Poetry and Letters

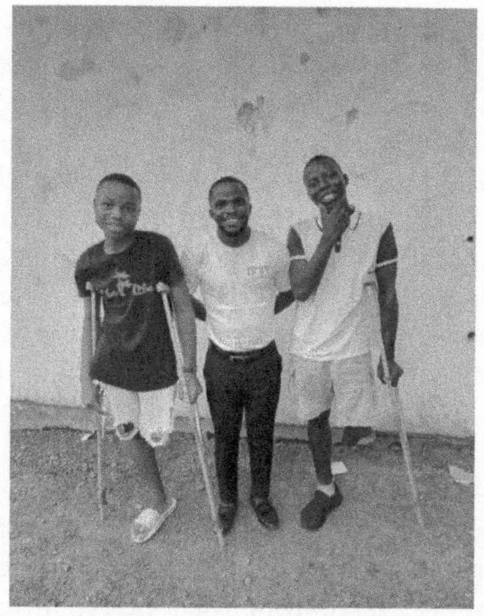

Geronimo, Jacob (Project Leader) and Ezekiel, in Liberia

Liberia – by Trustee Bronwen Hinton

Liberia is one of the least developed countries in the world. Approximately 16% of the population has some sort of disability and 99% of the people with disabilities live in extreme poverty. Only one third of primary school age children are enrolled in school.

People with disabilities face barriers such as stigma, inaccessible infrastructure, exclusion from education, are socially marginalised, there is above average unemployment, and generally high rates of illiteracy.

Currently we have 15 children enrolled in our programme ranging from 7–18 years old. They have a variety of amputations from below and above the knee, below and above the elbow to fingers and toes. Each child is given schooling, transportation to school, counselling, physiotherapy, prosthetics as required, crutches and constant support from our amazing Liberian Project Manager, Jacob. The children's education and health is constantly monitored and when necessary, the children are taken for life saving bone trimming operations on their residual limbs and their recovery is carefully managed. As our children are now reaching 18 we are looking at providing workshops for those leaving school to better prepare them for finding work.

Liberia's infrastructure is harsh for an able-bodied person let alone an amputee. We ensure the children on our programme are mobile, educated, and healthy and with our support have hope for a better future.

A Student Amputee – By Jacob Doe (Project Leader)

A student amputee
Born complete
Whole and full
Strong and focused
With my future in my bag

Life journey about to take
While uncertainties loom ahead
Here comes a day full of hope
Then darkness wholly crosses my path
Realizing that my leg is gone
Yet confident about travelling afar
Not deterred by criticism, but grateful
That Elizabeth's Legacy of Hope
Has been supportive
Pushed by neglect and frustration
Hopping on crutches with cord and sole palm
With the goal ahead that I may win
Though my story may be sad
Never do I attract pity to myself
But support as I receive from Elizabeth's Legacy of
  Hope
Not that my walls lie in shambles
Not that the journey is too far to travel
Not that my faith is broken
But that my pains are many
And that my strength is fading away
On tears I feed and only sorrow I know
Elizabeth's Legacy of Hope came as a helping hand
To save the life of a drowning kid
With education I hope and to smile
And walking again becomes a dream come true

Difficult to Accept – Ezekiel Tamba – age 17

It was very difficult to accept
Not that I was born amputated
But I had to accept my fate
After losing my leg.

My mother cried many nights
If tears could turn back the past
I would have had my leg now
My friends didn't just look down on me
But also made a fool of me.

I grew up playing alone
And it helps me to be independent
While my joy was being washed away
Elizabeth's Legacy of Hope came knocking
With fresh and new hope to hold onto
That I may walk again they built me a prosthesis
And with education they enlighten my hopes.

I may not be able to pay back
But the smile on my face
Shows how grateful I am

The Future – Moses Taran Nuah – age 15

Had I known what lies in the future
I would have saved a journey to sorry
It was a holiday my mother took me on, a vacation
Leaving Monrovia was an exciting moment
Only three years old
Living with a single mother was challenging
Mother went to the creek to wash our clothes
A hunter came from hunting
Placed his gun, loaded with shot
On the rock and went inside.
A toy my little brother knew
took the gun and shot my leg
Suffering and pains became my food.

Education I wished for but never had,
People thought I was a burden
And no family would accept me
Elizabeth's Legacy of Hope came as safe heaven
And gave me my missing leg
Ensured my quality education
Elizabeth's Legacy of Hope became my new parents
Ever since then I have been a happy child
Had I known what lies in the future
In hopes I would have believed.

Angie – by Attorus Myers, Father of Angie, aged 12

Angie with a heart full with love and joy about school
Got run over by a driver on her way to school
To save her life Angie's right leg got amputated
It was very difficult
Accepting her with the new condition
She could not go to school
Cried every night because of pains
Walking with crutches and falling with it
Was a nightmare for Angie
We could not afford to pay for an artificial leg
Angie would hide from her friends
Came home sat and cried all day
We supported her emotionally
Yet it was challenging
Faith had its way
Connected us to Elizabeth's Legacy of Hope
Through educational, health and welfare support

Elizabeth's Legacy of Hope
Has ignited hope and renews Angie's courage

Thanks for the care and love
Thanks for your assistance to children with disabilities
Angie is now confident about a bright future.

Elizabeth's Legacy of Hope
Has given Angie a new prosthesis
Walking again on both legs
A dream comes true for my daughter
God bless Elizabeth's Legacy of Hope.

Sense of Completion – by Abednego Nana – age 15

I was disowned by my father
I lived and struggled with my mother.
I had an experience
I would never forget
I was sent to call my brother
From across the road
I got hit by a hit and run driver
I later landed in the hospital
Only to get my leg amputated
I went through lot of pains as a child
I could not go to school because my mom ran out of money
I learn to walk with crutches
As a child I thought my leg would grow again
This thought helped me overcome insults from my peers
Realizing my leg would never grow made me cry
I felt sad many days
My thought of getting two legs
Did not die a natural death
Elizabeth's Legacy of Hope gives me a sense of completion

I went back to school through their educational
 support
Then I received a prosthesis that I may walk again
In wearing the prosthesis, I felt more pain
However, I am getting more super with it
I smile because you extended your loving hands
In supporting a child like me

Counting the Stars – by Yatta S. Kromah – age 12

Life becomes challenging at times
In a world that is made of beautiful opportunities
And gazing at the glittering blessings of the creator

The thought about a beautiful future
Fills the heart with peace
When your two feet are gone
And on your knees you walk

Living the opposite of life
Indeed life becomes challenging at times
Losing both my legs
Took away my joy and brought sorrow
Naming the challenges I experience
Would be counting the stars

If tears would restore my legs
I wouldn't have been tied on this floor
Being rejected is a cake I have to eat

Indeed life becomes challenging at times
No one would discomfort themselves for your comfort
Yet, in the arms of a loving mother I find love

In the support of Elizabeth's Legacy of Hope, I find courage

I will ignore the call of failure
I will succeed
I was born with greatness
And shaped differently
In hope there is life.

Letters from Liberia

Naomi Faigu, mother of 11-year-old Samuel

Let me acknowledge and appreciate the almighty God for his many blessings upon the life of me and my family. We the parents of Samuel Boakai are totally grateful to Elizabeth's Legacy of Hope for their consistent support to Samuel through the years. The support Samuel continues to receive has given him a reason to hope for a better life. Samuel takes his school work very seriously. We are also grateful to Jacob who has been very supportive in ensuring that Samuel is in school and has his prosthesis. In the midst of unemployment, it has always been difficult for us to give Samuel the support he needed as a child. When Samuel received his first prosthesis it was a dream come true for all of us. Today Samuel plays soccer with his prosthesis in fact he tries to do everything his friends do. Once again Thanks to Elizabeth's Legacy of Hope for keeping Samuel on this wonderful program.

John Togbah – Father of student Geronimo Togbah

I am happy to express my sincere thanks to Elizabeth's Legacy of Hope for supporting my son Geronimo Togbah. The situation that led to my son's amputation is a memory I will never forget. People in my community had too many negative things to say. Some of them said my wife and I were responsible for our son's misfortune. Geronimo's accident caused my family financial constraints and surviving his treatment was a nightmare. Every time I see my son walking with his prosthesis, I think it's a dream. Elizabeth's Legacy of Hope's support came just at the right time when I had gone totally broken and ever since then they have been a caring and very supportive organization. Through their support my son travelled to places and met new people. My family and I remain grateful and pray that God may continue to bless everyone that is associated with this organization.

Elizabeth's Legacy of Hope's Friends in Sierra Leone

Sierra Leone – by Trustee Victoria Panton Bacon

Located in the West Coast of Africa, next to Liberia, Sierra Leone is as beautiful a country as its neighbour, with stunning white beaches and lush forestation – but, like Liberia, it too is very poor, with most of its population of around 8 million people living below the poverty line. It has had a particularly troubled history in the last twenty-five years or so – around a third of its population were displaced and thousands of people were killed during the civil war in the 1990's. The bitter conflict eventually ended in 2002, bringing with it a more stable economy, but the destruction of many schools, hospitals and roads during the war made recovery slow; and just as it was starting to rebuild Ebola arrived in 2014, resulting in the deaths of more than 3,500 people – many more losing livelihoods.

These are two countries that cry out for support from international charities like Elizabeth's Legacy of Hope. We have a wonderful partnership in both Sierra Leone and Liberia with World Hope International, an American organisation who fund many humanitarian projects in poor and developing countries across the world. We have sixteen children we care for together in Sierra Leone – providing them with education, prosthetic, medical and all the holistic support that they need.

Letters from Sierra Leone

Sheku Sesay – from Mambureh Calaba Town

I was born normal, but I lost my limb the time I was involved in a road accident where it was broken. I was taken to a place where they treated me with herbs and at the end my limb started to decay and was very painful so they took me to the hospital where the advice was to amputate the limb. This is how I got amputated.

What I do to overcome stress is when I am with my friends playing football and when I study my notes and read stories. Pastor Finney also encourages me to study hard so that I can get a brighter future.

I want to thank ELoH and the ETC members for being so kind and giving me more hope for the future.

Daniel Kamara – age 13

My disability came as the mudslide happened at Regent on the 14th of August 2017 as I was trapped by the mud and was not conscious of things that happened around me. Everybody thought I was dead so they took me to the mortuary as a dead person. I thank God they noticed that I was still alive and moved me to the main hospital.

The way I manage stress is in school because my friends and teachers are always friendly and also any time I am visited by Pastor Finney or any of your team members because of the way you talk and encourage me that gives me hope for the future. At home my stepmother is also very kind to me and this helps me to overcome my worries.

I will like to say thanks to the World Hope, ETC, and ELoH for helping me so much

PART THREE: Poems of Courage

Smiling Bravely – Joanna Lumley OBE, Patron of Elizabeth's Legacy of Hope

When the world seems dark and gloomy
When you don't know what to say
When you're frightened, when you're lonely,
Know that it will be okay.

Walking slowly, breathing quickly,
Facing problems day by day,
Smiling bravely, please be hopeful,
Knowing it will be okay.

We're all in this boat together.
We shall chase your blues away.
Talk to someone, write to someone.
Knowing it will be okay

Undefeated – by Kathryn Beevor (Elizabeth's Legacy of Hope Trustee)

The dual-coloured jewel
Pink and black,
Perfect symmetry.
I could have picked you
From the jeweller's tray

A gem
One would be proud to wear.

I polished you with water
On my arm
I wondered at your clarity
Your tenacity.
A beauteous stone
Shining and rare
Precious and covetous.

Until one day I faced you
Tore your exquisiteness
From my skin.
Stick my tongue out at
Cancer
I won, not YOU.

Overcoming Adversity – Hughie Teape

Adversity is a tragedy that can hit you from out of the blue.
To overcome it, work to discover the things that you can do.

No matter who you are in life, adversity can come your way.
And when you go to tackle it, just aim to start without delay.
Commit to applying positive thinking as this will help you cope.
In order to move forward in life, you must believe there's hope.

So make sure you are always looking only on the bright side.
And just follow your gut instincts as this can be the right guide.
Having to deal with any adversity is such an enormous test.
And when you're being positive, you'll give it your very best.

You may well seek professional help and this is okay to do.
Then as you start progressing, just be sure to see it through.
Fighting with adversity leaves you swimming against the tide.
But all the lessons from your battles will then be on your side.

You will also need determination if you and adversity meet.
And then to finally overcome it means victory will be sweet!

Never Surrender – Ranulph Bacon (age 11)

When Britain was at war
It seemed we would lose, for sure
But then they swore –
Never Surrender

When a friend was dying
All you did was crying
But to their illness
They would never surrender

When your days are cold
Let the events unfold
Remain strong and bold
Never Surrender.

Grounded – Sue Hardy-Dawson

The tiny boy
In the wide wheelchair
Reaches out a hand
To the climbing bar
Though his hand is small
And the reach too far

His dreams are as tall as another's are
Eyes closed as he smiles
Then takes to the air
Far beyond the earth,
The moon, the stars

M-M-Murray's M-M-Mountains – Shauna Darling Robertson

Murray's a mountaineer
who's frightened of heights.

He lies awake nights
getting in frets
over summits and crests,

then scours the news
for tumbles and falls
and for ambulance calls.

He crawls on all fours
and combs the ground over
for lucky-leafed clovers
and st-st-st-stutters
like wind on a tent
before each ascent.

But then, event done
fear flouted, peak won
his valley-wide smile
could outshine the sun

Melissa – Shauna Darling Robertson

Then suddenly she smiled
and the day began again.

Where did that smile come from,
did it blow in from the street?

Everything about her
had been sad, tired,
defeated (almost).

But then –
clouds do part.
Winter, let be,
steps aside for spring

Nerd Strong – Melanie Korach

They called her a nerd
and said she was weak.
They said she was
too kind & a bit of
a freak.

They called her a nerd
& laughed at her style.
Yet she basked in
her nerdiness and sent
them a smile.

For she knew she was
cool & forever strong.
And she would rock out
her nerdiness her whole
life long.

No Matter – by Julie Stevens

No matter how far I travel
I'll carry luck in my pocket.

No matter how heavy my load
I'll water my flowers of hope.

No matter how great my fear
I'll fill it with all things sweet.

No matter how much it hurts
I'll warm my smiles some more.

No matter how hard my day
I'll give my dream a home.

Golden Wall – Siobhan De Mare

I am the seed that grew from hope
As the challenges called me
My inner voice spoke
A roaring ocean drowning inside
A rainbow of dreams, determination and pride

My golden wall protects me each day
Resilience and gratitude
Lead the way

I am the seed, that grew from love
I am the voice that confirms you are enough

I am the soul
Once battered and bruised
I am the heart
Some laughed at and used

I am the smile
That you can never steal
I am the self esteem
That has learnt how to heal

I am love and I am light
I am sleeping beside you
On your darkest night

Some Days – Sarah Ziman

Some days you score your fill of goals.
And some the pitch is full of holes
A heavy heart weighs strong folk down
But raise your head, and bear your crown
We can't be happy all the time
Each summit takes a lengthy climb
If I could give you just one gift
Then it would be this mindset shift:
A falling ball can still bounce back
And light shines through the smallest crack

Be a Lion – Neal Zetter

Be a lion not a mouse
Be a castle not a house
Be a banquet not a lunch
Be the pick of every bunch

Be an ocean not a stream
Don't be the milk but the cream
Be a boulder not a stone
Be unique and not a clone

Be a tall tree not a twig
Be gigantic not just big
Be a 'yes' and not a 'no' or 'might'
... and let your confidence ignite!

Brave and Me – Kate Williams

Bravery will smile, mile after mile.

Bravery will laugh at roadblocks in its path.

Bravery will stay, whatever's in the way.

Bravery will ride the roughest ocean tide,
leap the dreadful deep, stride the gaping wide.

I know because we go across that sea together,
through the roaring weather, Brave and me.

Bravery will shine – like a medal it'll shine:

Can you see?

I Wanna Be Me – by David Anderson

I don't wanna be a teacher's pet,
Or a worried puppy, outside the vet.
I wanna be free, to be me
I don't wanna be a left-behinder
Or round and fat, like an old egg-timer.
I just wanna say, 'it's okay to be me. I'm being brilliant

I don't wanna be a geeky swot
Or green school custard that looks like snot.
I wanna be free, to be me.
I don't wanna be last in the queue
Or a chimp with a limp, locked up in a zoo.
I just wanna say, it's okay to be me,
I'm perfectly unique.

I don't wanna be known as a loser
Or an old mobile phone, without any future.
I wanna be free, to be me.
I don't wanna be an instigator
Or a piping hot baked potato.
I just wanna say, it's okay to b me.
I'm a random genius

I don't wanna be the bully's victim
Or a frightened chicken, running round the kitchen
I wanna be free to be me.
I don't wanna be, nobody's second choice
Or a scared little bird, without a voice.
I just wanna say, it's okay to be me.
I'm a gift to this world.

PART FOUR: Inspired by India

India – by Trustee Kathryn Beevor

Elizabeth's Legacy of Hope extended its help to more child amputees when a partnership was established in July 2015 with HEAL, (Health and Education for All), a charity which supports orphaned and underprivileged children in India. The Elizabeth Panton Artificial Limb Centre is based at Paradise Village, Andhra Pradesh, where I visited in December 2019. The amputees attend the centre to receive their medical care and are looked after by a team of remarkable doctors and technicians.

They have access to a mobile Limb Clinic via the ambulance provided by our generous donors. I witnessed first-hand the joy of our amputees as they walk, run and dance, no longer feeling the stigma of disability or being shunned by society. I left humbled by our children's courage and spirit which made me more determined to continue the work of our charity for these youngsters and those yet to receive a prosthesis.

Durga Vaishnavi

When I see a bird flying in the air, I too felt like flying.
When I see a fish swimming in the water, I too felt like swimming.
When I saw a cuckoo bird on the branch of a tree, I felt like singing.
When I see a calf jumping behind its mother (Cow), I too felt like jumping
But, fate has made me lonely..., But, ...but. ELoH and HEAL has given me rebirth.
Now I am able to walk with an artificial limb. I am able to go on a bicycle and am able to dance now.
Thank you ELoH and HEAL

Karri Swathi

Our daughter who should have been an eyelid to us,
Our daughter who should have shined like the light of our house,
Has filled our eyes with tears and our hearts with distress
Being disabled not able to walk on her own

Not able to see her agony, we too cried,
In my daughter's life ELoH and HEAL have filled it with fresh rainy drops and a new ray of hope
By providing a new artificial limb, wiped our tears and distanced our distress
And filled our family with happiness

With thanks Karri Yesubabu, father of KarriSwathi

K.Ganga Raju

The tidal wave that has come in the family of yes, the poorest of the poor,
Has given troubled times to all the family members,
The one who should have uplifted the family has been crippled, .
The childhood had become lame and hope got vapourised,
Only distress remained, and at that hopeless state,
And ELoH and HEAL remained my strength
Has made the one who could not walk, walk again.

With thanks, K.Ganga Raju

Chinta Surekha

Like birds that fly in the sky,
Like the deer that jump here and there though I too wanted to run,
Fate had treated me differently and made me disabled
But God in the form of ELoH and HEAL has provided me an artificial limb
And made my hopes and imaginations for me come true
Sky is only the limit for my happiness

Anchita D

Beautiful childhood got crushed
The palanquin of one core hopes broke down
The twine that gives melodious sounds was broken,
The doll that should have been very carefully handled has become disabled
And unable to walk
From distress and disappointment lifted up ELoH and HEAL and started growing again
Small Achintha started going to school

With heartful thanks, D. Nagaiah father

Aakash V

Went out to bring medicines to Daddy,
Drunken truckdriver hit me, changed this
Though not lost life, the removed leg has made me unable to stand
Though the sticks on my either hands gave some support,
It became so difficult to walk on my own
ELoH and HEAL gave me strength and confidence
And is responsible for me to continue my studies.

Many thanks to ELoH and HEAL.

Letters from India

Guthula Mohini

My respects to the esteemed organization ELoH. I thought that I can never see this world with my eyes. Though I have eyes, I have no legs. I thought I can never fly in this world. ELoH has given me wings. I am able to go to my college with the legs given by ELoH without any difficulty and showed me the light of this world. I am able to enjoy my college life. When I thought that there is nothing I can do, this organization has shown me the way. This organization has given me as much confidence as my mother had given me.

Rayalla Sunitha

By birth my daughter was born dumb, deaf and disabled. In our lives without any hope, ELoH and Heal organization have given new hope by donating artificial limb to my daughter. Now my daughter is able to walk on her own and is studying for a degree. Our wholehearted thanks to you.

By Rayalla Nageswara Rao father of Rayalla Sunitha

riyanka T.

Disability means insult. Disability means one is a burden to oneself. Though I have hopes as anyone else, there is no hope that I will be able to reach them. Though I wanted to develop like others, yet, disability makes me immobile. In the lives without any hope, EloH and HEAL have filled light in my life for which I am grateful for ever.

PART FIVE: Poems to Lighten Darkness

At Night – by Terry Waite OBE

At night
When all is still
I dream.
My mind Flies through the darkness
Crosses the sparkling ocean
Lands on a foreign shore.
I run along the beach
Throw myself into the waves
My arms and legs move gracefully
As I glide through the water.
Someone calls my name
The dream vanishes
As my eyes open to greet another day.
I am lifted from my bed
I have no limbs to carry me.
Only my dreams
And the hope of a miracle.

The Mist of a Tiny Energy – William Drew-Batty

Along the road,
Out of hedges thick with protection,
Darting through sedge and thistle, cornflowers
Overgrown elder, over ruts hidden in the

Curved underlay of course grasses,
The tiny birds dart
As vengeful for life as the
Children of the world who risk
Life and limb
Crossing roads blind in their
Newly-charged days of eating time and
Never being full:
The right of all who live and fly.

And now the blackbird,
Young, fledgling-fast, skims the tapering blades
Dangerous to the ground and keeps ahead of my
Nearside wing; out of the verge, briefly teasing
Death,
Then immediately up and down into a hedge-gap,
Gone.

A mile further on, in the already daring heat of a
Summer desperate to claim that name,
There lies in the road something that once
Seized the day, flew without thought on
Wings now bloodied, folded hideously,
Crumpled and lost.

My car chases the aftermath of down,
Fluttering over my windshield,
A gentle descent, a brief eulogy,
As fragile as nothingness,
As light as a weightless thing;
The mist of a tiny energy that once was
But now trails my life like a reminder of living and
loss,
As if, without guilt, I had consumed it.

This Child – Willard McPherson (aka William Fergusson)

We don't know this child
Held by her mother, whose arms,
Tapering into a void,
May not caress since shorn
Of touch by envy's reckoning,
A sharp blast on a perfect morning.

We cannot know how she feels,
This child who gazes
into an exploding glass, a false
Eye recording unbearable pasts
And unknowable futures born of war;
War, whose stake is famed illusion,
Whose bounty, vain pride.

Yet from terror, fire and rubble,
And in her eyes wide,
We may see truth's instinct survive
And love's flames
More intensely burn, despite.
We know this child.

Merch Stall (For Sam) – Luke Wright

I sign the books and you collect
the cash. You're eight, as careful with money
as you are with love. Up and up it goes

as kind-eyed strangers hand you springy notes.
You tally-up our profit in your head and whisper
it to me. When the bell rings

and our punters drift away I tell you
ten pounds is yours to keep.
I turn and gather up the books. You fall silent

for a moment, counting in your head. I'm about
to clip the case shut when you stop me,
hold the tenner out, ask if you can buy a book,

and break the bloody bank.

Because I broke – Shauna Darling Robertson

The sun was strangled by the sky
because I broke
and the moon suffocated the stars.

The mountains cast shadows across the valleys
because I broke
and the woods hummed with a hollow moan
as the rivers burst their banks
with the grief of the world which,
because I broke,
was no longer needed.

The shops pulled down their shutters, nailed up signs –
broke.
Way out west all the cowboys dismounted,
the whole game up now because I broke.

(Through)

Today, when the sun rises it means it
because I broke
and shoots burst up thirsty from the ground.

So what if the waters are still glacial?
Because I broke
I am now my own wetsuit
and possess all the know-how needed to remake myself
as polar bear or seal.
Because I broke
I can dive / drink / float anywhere.

The people in the streets avoid each other's eyes.
I broke
and so I gaze unfazed into all their souls,
stark naked with compassion because I broke.

The Land of Blue – Laura Mucha

Across the valley, it waits for you,
a place they call The Land of Blue.

It's far and near, it's strange yet known –
and in this land, you'll feel alone,
you might feel tears roll down your cheek,
you might feel wobbly, weary, weak.

I know this won't sound fun to you –
it's not – this is The Land of Blue.
It's blue – not gold or tangerine,
it's dark – not light, not bright or clean.

It's blue – and when you leave, you'll see
the crackly branches of the tree,
the golden skies, the purring cat,
the piercing eyes, the feathered hat
and all the other things that come
when you escape from feeling glum.

Across the valley, it waits for you,
a place they call The Land of Blue
and going there will help you know
how others feel when they feel low.

If I lose my eyes – Ben Langley

If I lose my eyes would I see only darkness
And drown in the memory of this colourful life?
Or would I wake to tiptoe from my robe
And swim in the morning light?

Like a country in lockdown
What magic will appear?
What will I observe?
What will I regard?
What will I notice?
What will become clear?

PART SIX: Just Wrong ...

John Foster – They have blown my legs away

They have blown my legs away
They have blown my legs away.
They have cut my life in half.
The men who planted the mines
Say they acted on my behalf.

It doesn't really matter
What they were fighting for.
It's innocent people like me
Who pay the price of their war.

But it's people half a world away
Who should hang their heads in shame –
The people who made and sold the toys
That they used in their wicked game.

PART SEVEN: Poetry by Children, for Children, for whom we all are

These poems are by the children of Thorpe House School, in Buckinghamshire, where Elizabeth's Legacy of Hope Trustee Kathryn Beevor is an English teacher. The first few poems are all written with the theme of 'Hope.'

Thank you all!

Theo McCann, Year 8

Hope, it says it all in the name,
life without her will never be the same.
Day and night, Hope is there,
for every thought and every prayer.

A beautiful soul, now and forever,
Simply with the sight of a dainty feather.
Longing for her beautiful hair and beautiful smile,
Soon in the afterlife we will reconcile.

No longer being on this earth,
never lessens your absolute worth.
Remember, remember the 15th December,
The day we will always recall, a family with one less member.

Hope has a different meaning,
rather than a word or a feeling.
It is my sister that lives within me.

Throughout this year,
everyone has wept and moped.
Whereas my family
we have HOPE.

Tyrell Gardner, Year 7

A bright and sunny day in the month of May
Flags flying high in the wind
Supporters cheer so much to hear

The teams play fast, they're really trying
Half time, no score, there's more to come
The 2nd half played at the run

1 minute to go, still no goals
Down goes the striker, can't handle the pressure
Penalty to my team, it's me and my dream
90,000 people ... hope!

Mallik Fattouki, Year 6

What is hope?
We don't know if it's far or near
Where is hope?
It could be right there, or even here.

Hope is something you can't feel,
Is something you can't touch.

Really, if you think about it
Hope is nothing much

This is what hope seems,
a quandary if you will,
Hope seems a lot like this
But hope comes still.

Harry Watts, Year 5

Hope is a feeling, that helps you through the day.
Get through any struggling, fingers crossed it will go away.
The aspiration to succeed and to thrive,
Hope, wish, determined to strive,
With hope we will find the power,
We will get through it all, our finest hour.

Year 1 Collaborative Class Poem

I hope...
The annoying virus goes away
Then we can hug again one day

I hope...
The whole world can be healthy
And the poor become more wealthy

I hope...
There is more love everywhere
As in lockdown we learned to share.

Year 2 Collaborative Class Poem

We hope we get up to free readers one day,
And Santa delivers us books on his sleigh
We hope that pasta is always on the menu
When we get our pudding we always say thank you.

We hope for a cleaner planet one day
We hope Covid-19 isn't here to stay!
We hope there are no more oil spills
We hope the toucans are safe in Brazil.

We hope that school never ends
And we never have to say goodbye to our friends
We hope we grow up smart and strong and that our lives are fantastic and long

Lockdown – Kayan Patel, Year 3

2020 is a scary time,
So I thought I'd write this little rhyme,

With lockdown in so many places,
Missing people's lovely faces,
Granny and Grandad can't see me,

Mum said "safety is the Key!",
Weekends filled with Disney Plus,
Stops us making such a fuss!

One Day, remember this little rhyme,
Keep hoping for a happier time.

Rescue Racer – Julius Pietrek, Year 4

Rescue Racer zooms to space
Carting tonnes of human waste
Mission target, blazing sun
Leaving Earth, to have more fun.

No more cars, speed pods here
Pollution gone, have no fear!
Pod bikes zooming all around
Planet Earth, safe and sound.

Hurtful weapons have no place
Humans are an awesome race.
Caring and loving more and more,

Sharing better than ever before.

Never Give up! – Ryan Degan, Year 3

I ride a bike
For the first
Time.

Fall off! You
Want to quit
But your mum comes along

Your mum
Said, "Don't give up".

Fly High – Geraint Jones Year 3

Fly high like a plane.
Don't go low like the snow.
Go fast like a F1.
Don't go slow like a gnome.
Feel like the sun and not the
Rain and you can do anything.

Bicycle – Viren Dhaliwal, Year 4

So thin wheels
No stabilisers now
I'm so scared.

It's like a monster on my bed
"I'm scared!"
I said.

My dad's holding on
He said,
"I'm at the end of the road."

"Wait how do I brake?
Aahhhhhh! I'm scared!"
I said.

Wait, Dad's on
The other side
Of the road.
"I'm riding a bike!"

I said.
"Hi," my dad shouted,
"YaY!" I said.

The Late Night Lake – James Barton, Year 4

I came across a lake
And it was very late
I can't swim
Whatever will I do?
I will learn.
Stay confident.
Be strong.
When I reach the other side
It will put a smile on my face
And fill me with grace.
And that is the magic of the late night lake.

Practice – Oscar Wood, Year 7

Practice makes perfect
Just like flour makes a cake.

Practice makes perfect
Just like the moon makes the night

Practice makes perfect
Just like the sun makes a smile
You don't need to be perfect,
You need to be yourself

OCD – Oliver Tait, Year 7

Don't let it control you,
Control yourself,
Do what you want to do,
If you control it,
You win,
But that's only the start, there is so much more to overcome.

My First Feel at Professional Football – Rory Wallwork, Year 8

As I step put onto the pitch
A glimmer of light shines down
Crowds cheering, drums banging
Nerves jangling,
New life is breathed into my soul
Feeling holes in my heart,
But confidence flying.

Something I'll never forget
Playing for Tottenham,
This is where I shine or flop,
On the highest stage
I sacrificed a lot
But have been rewarded by heaven
At eleven pm, the latest of times
I score a goal and it all kicks off!
Beers being thrown, and crowds cheering
The best moment of an incredible life
Begins!

Goal – Oscar Wolfe, Year 8 (To my Grandad)

Tho he breathed
His last breath
He would say to me
None of the less

It don't matter
If you're big or small
Be what you want
Put your goals up tall.

Do not be scared
If you're different from others
Grab that goal
Like the hand of your mother.

You can play
Rugby or football
Don't give up!
Just work hard in school.

My Dad – Tom Milburn, Year 4

My dad is hope,
My dad is life,
My dad is funny,
My dad.

My dad is brave,
My dad is strong,
My dad is smart,
My dad.

Fear Shall not Stand! Jack Langlands Year 4

Fear shall not stand.
Never at all,
Stand up strong,
Don't worry if you get it wrong.

Be yourself,
Don't let bad things get into your head.
Hope is there,
And will conquer fear.

PART EIGHT: Special Collection – Poetry with Legs, by Patron Ian Whybrow

Ian Whybrow has written over a hundred books for children and is a patron of ELoH. He writes:

The pandemic put a stop to my going into schools to talk about my books for children and incidentally to raise money for ELoH. Halfway through July 2020, I decided to write a poem a day for a year in the hope that people might sponsor the effort – even if poems are not their cup of tea. When the year was up and my little marathon had made a surprisingly large sum for the charity, I found I couldn't stop. I still can't. So now I'm aiming to keep going for at least two years.

I've chosen – from the hundreds I've written so far – some poems that praise and celebrate little, private pleasures in life, even in sad or trying circumstances and remind us of the amazing capacity of everything in nature to keep going and often to cheer us up. In "The Frog Princess" I drew on a well-known fairy story to try to get to the heart of what a little girl might suffer after losing a leg. I felt sure there would be a lot of anger and blame. Mostly she would blame herself and want to hide away. She would be sure to feel ugly and a useless burden to her family. Other children would say cruel things about her. In a poor country, it would be hard for her to get medical help, to go to school, to get a job – or to have any fun. And that's where ELoH comes in – bringing hope and practical help.

Long may it flourish!

Ian W.

July 18th, 2020 – Your bathwater

It isn't simply economy
that makes your bathwater such a joy
but perhaps that I am normally
an amateur of the shower.

I find it takes the weight off me
and ripples me into strange and interesting shapes.
Sometimes a brunette sea anemone surfaces
between my pale old-chap breasts
and the islands of my knees.

My shipwrecked toes
rise like a warning
to the ghosts
of our children's floating bath-toys.

I love to pull out the plug and feel
myself slowly flattened to the thickness
of a non-slip mat
which in our case we have not got.

July 19th, 2020 – Drive-thru swab

Keep forgetting about this bloody visor
she says, flapping it down with a green-gloved hand
over the masked smile
I could hear was there.

I, nervously parked in Bay A
outside a small canvas pavilion
in the hospital car park,
press the window-down button.

Can't see a dicky bird in the rain
she tells me.
You alright darling? This won't be very nice.

It goes down both sides of your throat
then up both nostrils.
There we are. Whoops. Must be all that wine last night.

Life goes on, then.

July 24th, 2020 – A charm against tight pants

I have found a new purpose for
chests of drawers.
Stretch your tight underpants
between any two handles
not for the same drawer
and you will find
you can now slide into them
in comfort.

Not the drawers
but the drawers.

July 29th, 2020 – A hope (Sweet Peas Red)

You were 98 when your arthritis stopped you
baking cakes for me and not long after that
you were dead.
I thank you for saving these sweet pea seeds
and leaving them for me instead.

I have put them in water
before I put them in earth tomorrow.
I hope they will rise up, Joan,
rise up, Joan, and perfume the air
in this house that you loved.

When the pandemic has gone
and we bring your ashes to
scatter on the Gower Peninsula
we shall stop here in Herefordshire
and lay a small part of you in the garden,
with (I hope) your sweet peas.

August 10th, 2020 – Hovering

"*To deal with a bee or butterfly trapped against a window, place an upturned tumbler or cup over it, slide a card gently under the vessel and release the creature outside.*"

What are you thinking?
crepe-winged hoverfly
soaring from upturned cup
back to the sky?

You thought my windowpane
was toughened light?
The cup a prison?
Sliding postcard, night?

Were you excited
by escape, ascent –
or is just anywhere
your element?

August 20th, 2020 – Praise for Emily Dickinson

There is no hope of knowing what she meant –
only that hope for her was feather-sent.
She was a loaded gun, though, that's for sure.
Thank God that someone looked behind her door.

September 10th, 2020 – Ideal

You are perfect, o banana!
Daily this is how I feel
about the way you fit my hand,
about the easy way you peel.

No artisan makes artisana
to equal thee, ideal banana!

October 30th, 2020 – Small jobs to do in the garden this week…

Check in the shed for things you do not need;
dig them well in and let them go to seed.

Think about seeds you'd really like to grow
and let them flourish in your mind right now.

Scrub out the pots that grew resentments.
Plant up some bulbs that promise you fragrance,

ideally in re-usable bulb planting trays.
Seek out some of the many handy ways

to use up beetroot and the chunks of hake
you freezered in the days of Hereward the Wake.

December 1st, 2020 – Just now

Just now
I raised the blinds to see
the moon caught in the chestnut tree.
Lit from within
it shows its embers through its skin

and now again

up and to its right
another miracle of light
sits in a twig's fork
like a puffed-on spark.

Soon,

when smouldering star
and glowing moon ignite
they'll scorch away
this rumpled papery night.

December 3rd, 2020 – O, clivea!

O, clivea
how generous you are!
Trussed, under-watered,
over-wintered in the downstairs lav
and *still* you flower!

December 12th, 2020 – Mrs God and her hobbyist husband

He's in the shed,
shouldn't be long.
He's got some stuff
he's working on.

He calls it time.
Yes, hard to explain.
Think of weather
with no sun or rain.

Or a lavender bag
without the lavender
tucked away
inside a drawer.

Only he's made
a bigger place
to keep it in.
He calls it space.

I call it the cart
before the horse.
Bang! Here we go –
another universe!

January 4th, 2021 – Hello, Aloe

O cactus,
with more legs than an octopus;
we never liked you but you've stuck it out here.
So after what we've been through together
– you on just the odd spoonful of water –
we want you to persevere.
Please count yourself one of us.

March 12th, 2021 – The Frog Princess

For all the child amputees helped by
Elizabeth's Legacy of Hope

After the explosion I liked it in the dark.
I liked the drip and plop
and the river smell
you get from being down a well.

I didn't call out.
Alone, I was content.
I felt I deserved
my punishment.

The dark was my shield
I would lie under it and stare
feeling my safety
in despair.

I heard you sing
of an end to pain,
how I might be beautiful
and useful again.

You dropped a rope
and told me not to worry.
If I'd let you, you would pull me up
but there was no hurry.

I did not believe a word you said
but that was a start.
I began to feel around in the mud
for the pieces of my broken heart.

March 25th, 2021 – Giving back

A boy who has lost his leg, Vusikila Rahul
lives somewhere almost half the graspable
world away, beyond where local feeling is involved.
He had no hope his problem could be solved.

His eyes say: Look. *I'm standing. This is me.*
And just as eloquent is his poetry.
To give a person back a means to make a living
with dignity; is there any better kind of giving?

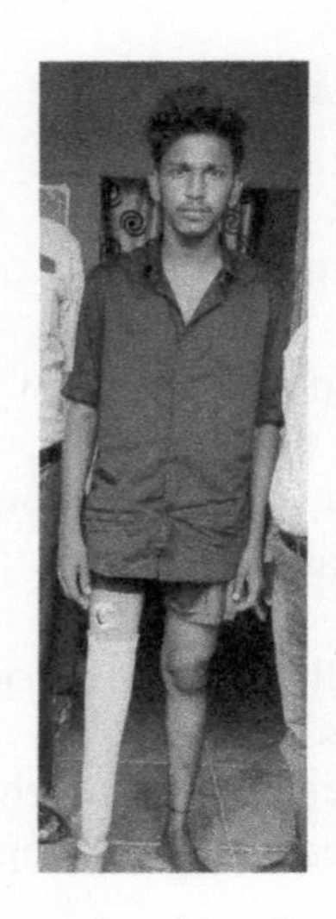

"*We cannot imagine what befalls*
in our lives.
You can take the charred remnants
and we construct a life
unimaginably richer
from the shards and pieces that fell.
ELoH and HEAL gave me a second life.
Thank you very much."

Vusikila Rahu

April 18th, 2021 – No cuckoo

Out early with my cup of tea;
the birds call out from every tree
but no cuckoo.

Warbles and whistles, faint to-wu;
delight from every point of view
but no cuckoo.

Woodpigeons bubble throatily
I'm NOT Wayne Rooney. So I see.
Still no cuckoo.

The collared dove's sad triple-coo
is in the vein but will not do;
it's no cuckoo.

A cockerel without a clue
trumpets until his face is blue,
yet no cuckoo.

A distant cow heaves out a moo
as if she's yearning for you, too.
Come on! Cuckoo!

June 17th, 2021 – Quick work

I saved a spider from the sink
and blew it out the window.
It abseiled groundward in a blink.
I never saw one spin so.

August 15th, 2021 – A wish for my great-grandchildren

I should like us to meet
in a meadow
with grasshoppers
flying like sparks
hammered off
a red-hot horseshoe.

I should like to take off
my shirt
and hold it out
like a net
and dive among
the swaying grasses

to catch the sound
grasshoppers
used to make
and put it
in a jam jar for you
to believe in

and when you
all have the sound
firmly in your heads
I should like you
to let it go
and years later

when you think
you might be getting old
to catch it in a poem
for your great-grandchildren
and take it to a meadow
and listen to it with them.

September 6th, 2021 – I talked to that old lady

I talked to that old lady,
the one we used to see
out taking long runs.

Yes, tall and very skinny,
stares ahead seriously…
Poor thing's got Parkinson's!

That's where she lives, right up there.
There, up on the top floor.
See the striped deckchair

by that door that's wide open
and the pot with the tree in?
Okay that's her.

First time she's had to stroll
holding a walking pole.
Keeps falling over

she told me. Gave me her
name. I watched her stagger
off – Kate – on her walk.

Next time I happen to see
her I'll ask her to drop by
for a proper talk.

Epilogue

by Sean Allerton, Ambassador of Elizabeth's Legacy of Hope

Being asked to write an epilogue to these poems and being the other bookend to Lord Hague of Richmond's (a fellow Yorkshireman) thought-provoking Foreword, was a surprise to say the least. I can't comment on the technical aspects of any poetry, but I do recognise the emotion in the words within this collection.

I wasn't aware of Wilfred Owen's "Disabled" until I read about it in the Foreword, and thanks to the power of Google I now am, and can fully respect how anyone could be awed by Owen's words. Owen was writing in a different time; people today are much more understanding of disability in everyday life, so the emotion in Owen's line "*Tonight he noticed how the women's eyes, Passed from him to the strong men that were whole*" should no longer be felt, or anywhere as much – but it is. It isn't just how people see disability, but how a person with that disability may feel how they are perceived by others.

The work of Elizabeth's Legacy of Hope gives the amputees, amongst the other services they provide, the chance to be seen by their community, and feel it themselves, that they are not passed over, that they have the ability to be themselves and not just the burden they may feel that they are. Hopefully you will feel the emotion in the poems, and succinctly noted by Yatta S. Kromah in Section Two of this collection, that "On the support of Elizabeth's Legacy of Hope, I find courage".

Do find hope within this collection, let the words speak for the actions of Elizabeth's Legacy of Hope and the work it does, feel better in knowing you've helped others by buying this book, and know that by getting this far you've helped improve a child's life – probably more than you can ever imagine.

****

Note from Victoria, Trustee and ELoH Founder – about Sean:

I asked Sean Allerton if he would kindly consider being an Ambassador for ELoH two days after I first met him in the summer of 2015, at a gathering for Royal Air Force aircrew veterans from the Second World War (we both share an interest in WWII history).

Sean is wheelchair bound – he lost the use of his legs, and more, in a motorcycle crash in 1993 aged 28 whilst serving in the RAF Regiment when he was stationed in Cyprus. He told me, briefly, about his injury – but also how it has taught him to make most of every day he has. He told me, too, about how he raises funds for RAF charities, 'pushing' for many miles in his chair, along runways and around airfields at different RAF stations. To date he has covered 2200 + miles, also now raising money for Elizabeth's Legacy of Hope. He plans to 'push' for as long as he is able.

Sean is reticent when I thank and praise him for what

he does, always turning the thanks back on me, telling me how grateful he is that I asked him to be our Ambassador. Neither does he like it very much when I describe him as "Amazing, brave, inspiring, humble, courageous – etc." But Sean is all of these things, and far more. He sets humanity a wonderful example. I am glad he has let me use those words for the purpose of this book, just this once.

On behalf of the children, we are so grateful to you.

Victoria

Disabled – by Wilfred Owen

He sat in a wheeled chair, waiting for dark,
And shivered in his ghastly suit of grey,
Legless, sewn short at elbow. Through the park
Voices of boys rang saddening like a hymn,
Voices of play and pleasure after day,
Till gathering sleep had mothered them from him.

About this time Town used to swing so gay
When glow-lamps budded in the light-blue trees,
And girls glanced lovelier as the air grew dim,—
In the old times, before he threw away his knees.
Now he will never feel again how slim
Girls' waists are, or how warm their subtle hands,
All of them touch him like some queer disease.

There was an artist silly for his face,
For it was younger than his youth, last year.
Now, he is old; his back will never brace;
He's lost his colour very far from here,

Poured it down shell-holes till the veins ran dry,
And half his lifetime lapsed in the hot race
And leap of purple spurted from his thigh.

One time he liked a blood-smear down his leg,
After the matches carried shoulder-high.
It was after football, when he'd drunk a peg,
He thought he'd better join. He wonders why.
Someone had said he'd look a god in kilts.
That's why; and maybe, too, to please his Meg,
Aye, that was it, to please the giddy jilts,
He asked to join. He didn't have to beg;
Smiling they wrote his lie: aged nineteen years.
Germans he scarcely thought of, all their guilt,
And Austria's, did not move him. And no fears
Of Fear came yet. He thought of jewelled hilts
For daggers in plaid socks; of smart salutes;
And care of arms; and leave; and pay arrears;
Esprit de corps; and hints for young recruits.
And soon, he was drafted out with drums and cheers.

Some cheered him home, but not as crowds cheer
Goal.
Only a solemn man who brought him fruits
Thanked him; and then inquired about his soul.

Now, he will spend a few sick years in institutes,
And do what things the rules consider wise,
And take whatever pity they may dole.
Tonight he noticed how the women's eyes
Passed from him to the strong men that were whole.
How cold and late it is! Why don't they come
And put him into bed? Why don't they come?

Acknowledgements

In no particular order, the following people (and groups of people) must be thanked, most heartily, because the coming together of *Elizabeth's Poetry of Hope* has been a wonderful and complete collaboration. So, **THANK YOU** very much to:

All the poets! Many of you have written something special and original, especially for this book. Without your fine words there simply wouldn't be a book – thank you for the time, thought and care you have given, and for the empathy too that resonates throughout the book.

The ELoH team: Patron Ian Whybrow who has helped immeasurably with this book, whilst continuing to write a poem every day for two years – to raise money for *ELoH* (nothing short of amazing!) Trustees Bronwen Hinton, Kathryn Beevor, Judy Moorhouse and Susanne Russell – you all do so much

'Bookends!' Lord Hague of Richmond and our Ambassador Sean Allerton for the moving and thoughtful Foreword, and Epilogue.

On the production side: Clays Printers in Bungay, notably Paul Hulley for his generosity and Isabel Hinchin for her advice; David Francis at RefineCatch for the typesetting; and Kerry Timewell for the lovely front cover illustration.

Thank You All

Finally, I mention in the Introduction to this book that *Elizabeth's Poetry of Hope* is, in part, to celebrate *Elizabeth's Legacy of Hope's* tenth anniversary which was in May 2021. So many people have done so much to ensure we reached this amazing milestone – **thank you** if you have been part of our journey – fundraising, donating, sponsoring – we wouldn't be continuing to care for our child amputees without you.

Thank you too, to all our Patrons and Trustees who have done so much: Patrons Simon Eccles, Hugh Monro, Joanna Lumley, Roland Rudd, Richard Bacon and Timothy Briggs; and former trustees Kevin Craig, Rebecca Newsome, Jennie Evans, Georgina Jarrett, Sarah and Christopher Hope (also Founders of *ELoH*.)

Thank you too to our care-givers and partners in each of our chosen countries, without whom our support for the child amputees would not exist; the staff of World Hope International in Sierra Leone, Liberia and at their headquarters in America, at Health and Education for All in India; and thank you to our previous partners Street Child, Williette Safehouse and Friends of the Children of Tanzania.

Finally – last, but certainly not least – the children we care for. It is immensely rewarding and heartening to read your words of gratitude in your poems and to know we can help you. **Thank You.**

It is wonderful that Elizabeth's Poetry of Hope has come together. THANK YOU ALL. Enjoy every word!

Victoria Panton Bacon, co-Founder and Trustee